SCAR revision

tracy ryan

'Scar revision' — surgically minimising the
effects of scars — is the powerful central image
of Tracy Ryan's highly accomplished new
collection. Both formally adventurous and
movingly personal, these poems offer vivid
accounts of how we survive and 'rewrite' literal
and symbolic scars, and of regeneration
through the risks of family.

*Tracy Ryan's poems are tightly packed vibrations
of spiky conceits. They have a restless intelligence
which seems to suspect everything they touch; the
references are scholarly and the contention is
feminist but the result is polychromatic.*

Tim Allen, *Terrible Work* (UK)

T0363352

Tracy Ryan was born in Western Australia but has also lived in England and in the USA. She has worked in libraries, bookselling, editing and community journalism, and has taught at various universities. She is especially interested in foreign languages and translation. She has two children.

Killing Delilah
Fremantle Arts Centre Press, 1994.

Bluebeard in Drag
Fremantle Arts Centre Press, 1996.

Vamp (a novel)
Fremantle Arts Centre Press, 1997.

Slant
rempress, 1997.

The Willing Eye
Fremantle Arts Centre Press, 1999.
Bloodaxe, 1999.

ex opere operato
vagabond, 2000.

Jazz Tango (a novel)
Fremantle Arts Centre Press, 2002.

Hothouse
Fremantle Arts Centre Press, 2002.
Arc, 2006.

bloc notes
equipage, 2007.

SCrevisionAR

tracy ryan

FREMANTLE
PRESS
fine independent publishing

For all my family

Contents

Acknowledgements

Some of these poems were first published in *The Age, Agenda, The Best Australian Poetry 2007* (ed. John Tranter), *The Georgia Review, The honey fills the cone: Newcastle Poetry Prize Anthology, 2006, Island, The Kenyon Review, The Literary Review, Poetry Review, Salt, Southerly* and *Westerly*.

Scar Revision

1.

At first I say: I have only three

but one scar leads to another and they
surface to memory
chainmail,
    piecemeal,
 like
a lost dream coming together,

each little marker caught,
geological,
though there is only one layer
and all times imprint there

proffered like fossils
or runes
inscrutable without context
without gloss

no working out by
internal logic
a writing
utterly private —

when I die they will last at least
as long as the rest of me

but keyless
yours too

until they disperse, the earth
indifferent to
detail in tissue.

2.
This from a chisel they call
gouge or *veiner*
in the heart of the left index
fingerprint

even the thought
triggers a tingling

interference in the
organic pattern

didn't know what the
right hand was doing

slippage or
self-sabotage

lulled by the soft surface
of pinewood
a moment's distraction

and suddenly
a rift in the flesh continuous
with the ruined carving

rift I saw blossom
like Aaron's rod with the red

promise of its own
overextension.

I stood outside
pain for that split
second before nerve
connects with brain

that interruption, a switch
to the image in negative

and back again,
the darkness forgotten.

3.
This from the murk
of a summer's estuary

diving in search of
something else
and missing the obvious —

the jetty concealing
its thousand shells
tight-lipped and honed

for grazing foot, for transient
body to generate
its answering lesions
in the way people once thought barnacles
engendered by wood that bore them.

The foot grew swollen.
The murk crept up the vein
like the red in a cheap thermometer,
a royal road,
an inside job.

The body wavered,
retracted,
    stood.

4.
Front of the left thumb a small pearl

though it dulls yearly
in a crosshatch of further wrinkles
losing distinction

caught in a bicycle bell
thirty years ago
the trivial
    still the most visible.

5.

… an intensity some would find overwhelming …

(obituary)

The one I can't see
or feel, on my left or right
shoulder, as if someone brushed there
and vanished

again a hot summer, when damage
just seems to happen or skin
is barest —

fourteen, the one Christmas party
ever held by my unhappy parents, the one boy
who will die young
                 of cancer
one day when we have both
almost forgotten each other
but who for now
holds my full attention and me squeezing small as I can
into a corner dragging the Exposed Clinker Brick
Interior along the length of me,
not even noticing, not even noticing I will go on.

6.

The ones I don't know I have,
the ones before language

that were not taught me
like memories learned from photos

the ones I mistake for blemishes
ones wasted on me

the ones I think I have
that are really someone else's

where my grandmother fell at nine
and hit her forehead
while stealing berries

where I placed my unmarked finger
as she told me at eighty

or the one I can feel but can't
locate, where they tore
my brother from me.

7.
Front and back are deliberate
interventions, professional,
planned, conversations held
about but
without me, notations to a future
surgeon I wish not to meet, an appointment
I don't want.

8.
Like automatic writing
so much of us is
involuntary these
should not surprise

flesh under instruction
we can't intercept

whatever is at work here
inserting
editing out.

9.
Or to light us
useless as tomb objects

a burial text
upon which none
may elaborate

each pucker and ridge
a cartouche of
self-reference

Rosetta-less.

10.
They are rope thrown out
a fallback
an afterthought
a second-rate —

without gland or follicle
incorporate Other.

It is said they can never
be removed completely

as if the body
will have its say

resistant to the end.

Snow baby

Gem in a dead setting

islet in a topographical blank
that laps the very steps
& stops rigid, propping the house up

where we are fixed for weeks,
microcosm.

A house full of give & creak
shed petticoats
dirty white
mise-en-scène
a has-been

you grace with beginning
gaze unfolding
daily a little further

dark flower
spreading ink

pool that broadens
with thaw, shrugging off edges

claiming the elements:

this churlish cold
only your foil, hot bundle

you reconcile
inside & out

bud-tight
corm clocking up knowledge
patient as night, you are

breath pressed by force
through the chink
in blue lips, you are the stamp

of features covered over
long since & uncannily
brought home, brought back.

Monitor

Your exhalations spread around the house —
I hear your vital signs as once you heard
my rhythms from inside. Like loved music
whose every cadence is familiar
and waited for, your breath upon the night
sings me to sleep. Sometimes it turns to talk,
and I can only guess at what you dream —
clock   car   dog   bird, the markers that by day
you fling at your surroundings, now become
a paratactic stream, as if the mouth
were under compulsion to continue
regardless of the mind and of the dark.
Sometimes a testing cry will call me in
should you lurch up in shock, to teach you how
to sink again, my brave submariner.
Could I still hear that with the naked ear?
This lifeline, my reverse umbilicus,
sign of a cyborg love, extends my reach
even as senses fade — the more I slip
the more I grasp, and turn the volume up.

Confluence

for my small child

Faces known or reported
who never met in life, meet here
in yours, in expressions
divested of context:
his heavy-lidded drinking
her rippling mischief —

all speak like lines
you haven't mastered yet
or clothes that fit but have not
worn in, the way palms are
already sketched but yet to weather.

Blood dowry in multiple
you'll spend or save
invest somewhere
or disown: unpredictable.

Meanwhile, guileless
you present this manifold aspect
as utterly continuous.

The eye flinches
the heart falters
as other life flickers
across your features.

This reaction too
you are watching:
seeking direction
in my countenance.

Softfall

1.   Grasp

Second-guesser, forestaller, laying my life's cloak out
in a useless gesture for your small feet to step over;

spinner, wrenching protective gossamer
from her own inner fibre, a barrier

of sorts and in certain dimensions, as if I could ache
with permanent milk and that proved anything

after weaning, a coating, a buffer, edge-beveller, rug-straightener,
fool-proofer, airbrusher, mind extending

a feeler, ahead of you, ontological
recapitulator, faithful retainer, overprogrammed

incubator, K-selected,
non-relinquisher. And yet

you grow bigger —
I weed each drawer as your frame

escapes me, replenishing.
I never keep up.

2. *Gravity*

Watching you fall in the same way twice is
a lesson on the limits of
language —

speechless, I only cradle your head and try
sounding it, depthless, with binary options like
does it hurt a *little* or a *lot?* — and so far you're
too truthful to choose what will please.

Still I go on, issuing words like so much
netting or wadding, that will eventually, the theory goes,
come in some stable way between you and the
hard ground.

3. *Amphibian*

After a bath, slippery pup, tadpole, you love to
torment me, as you think, by hiding
face under towel — *Say,*
Where's my little boy? Where is he? Where can he be?

in your ecstasy often forgetting
the punchline, the self-revelation.

You would lie there for hours
kicking those new frog legs,
naked and cold, but for the veiled face,
if I didn't curtail this.

4.   'To Earthward'

The way you crave
to meet the dirt, lock horns with it,
head-butting,
birth-urge in the wrong direction,
or diving as if you took land
for water. Even when burrowing into
your father on the sofa, you call it
the cave, his body
half the world's body, future to
your own. First day
in the new sandpit you stuff
your mouth with it, grinding
white teeth on white grit, your joy
hysterical — nothing I do
can wean you off it. *Munch on, crunch on*
you keep yelling, unwitting
in your quotation
from the *Pied Piper*
of Hamelin.

5.   *Bruiser*

I watch each one in turn
on your forehead
change size and colour

as if
predicting weather

part science, part superstition,
the repetition

of old wisdom. *It will blow over.*
I make you face the sun,
then turn, to check dilation.

But you look past me, mere
bystander, tender with ice-pack,
cold flannel, soft restricting
limbs, sad ballast

you want no part in:
I'm all right, Mum.

Tagging his clothes

It's like writing lines
for punishment

or learning lines, my latest
role, this repetition,

little variant
on my own signature
the hand wants to fall back on,

so I stick to full capitals, square
as an architect's, formal
as a cartouche

like learning to use
a married name
or resume the maiden one,

pain
in modification.

Pain of nuance, new usage
sending him forth like this
where a name is needed,

into the outside
where others will learn him,
hiving him off.

Thin strips I weld
when the iron is hot
to familiar items,
my grafting skin,

my styptic pencil,
my cauterising.

Torndirrup

I don't like it when things are smooth.
I want everything spiky
       — bipolar patient

1.   The Gap

Once an ur-continent,
now a lost line of connection
facing Antarctica

like the place of our own divide
we tread warily.

Years of the sea's rage
and abeyance
have worn away stone and patience.

We link at the elbow,
paper dolls
that bulk and slacken
in the wind's horizontal,

the way she must face
everything: braced, shored —

O the mind, mind
has mountains

so we inch toward
the parapet
that fools no one,
tiara on obstinate forehead.

She glances downward
and back
like someone sipping —
too hot, but drawn to it

then pats my hand
as she did in babyhood, at her limit.

Above us the hill
is black from fire, stopped only from leaping
by a narrow road

I read: turmoil and devastation,
the edge I must hold her back from.
She has been here before
but as usual, forgotten.

2. *The Natural Bridge*

Eventually, so the sign says
will become another Gap.

This stone has the contours of flesh
under strain,
hanging in there.

A balancing act.
Faith between gritted teeth.
Capricious with squeezed boulders,

Sisyphus, Atlas, I heroize
our endeavours.

There is no one to help us
but ourselves, this configuration
of stresses.

If I show any fear, she will crumble.

A tourist has crossed the rocks
with the zest and hubris
of youth, to jump, to stamp on the bridge

and make faces at her boyfriend
who screams from the railing.

We hold our breath,
my daughter in fascination.

3. *Jimmy Newell's Harbour*

They don't know who he was —
there were two of him
so the signs tell both versions

wavering as this weather,
hot, with a high wind,
labile and dangerous.

The cliffs are unstable,
you cannot swim there —
only look down from a platform
on satin perfection

stagy as dreams

and imagine
how it would feel
without the damaged patches

the managed vista
like pictures of heaven
when I was little

or the fantasy-futures
we plan for our children

before the slow erosion, life
sets in.

First Burn

All day she has pitched dry grass, Hardyesque,
perched on the stack, helping to raze the block
in a race against shire deadlines: fire risk.

Only her colours are wrong — curls a stark
hedge in English autumn, young fragile skin
dead-of-winter white. But she *will* work

to feel she's useful, wanting to fit in,
all my cautions thrown to the easterly,
hot from the desert. I've done all I can —

this is the point, the moment beyond me
for which we've struggled, locked like Gabriel
and Jacob, though the outcome may not be

a blessing. She is tall and capable,
strong on the outside — surely that's enough.
To look at her now no one else could tell

what tinder, what touchwood she was made of.
By evening there appears a subtle glow
upon her shoulders, imprinted as if

someone had held her fast; by morning so
reddened and furious she is aflame
with reproaches, and cries: *You made me go*

to England and then you made me come home.
Non-sequitur, she knows, but all the same
I am the mother, I must wear the blame.

Love knot

Sifting and digging through years of paper like
so many repeating autumns — old faxes fading, letters
brown at edges — for someone else altogether,
I find your hair,

not the everyday grey shed on pillows,
in shower drains, but a snipped token, back
when it was still black,
stapled and labelled, three months before
we were married.

A large curl, tied like a string-reminder,
like the ring I don't wear, but dark and bright
as our beginning. Tucked
in an airmail envelope, no destination,
the same way we later kept
our baby's first clipping.

Too big for a locket, too soon
for bracelet about the bone — I'd swear
someone else must have cut it,
but my own handwriting insists. Forgotten,
yet I have stayed true to it, unseen
as a scapular, sole jewel
sewn into the lining.

Sonnets after the Portuguese

… it is my spirit that addresses your spirit; just as if both had passed through the grave, and we stood at God's feet, equal, — as we are!
      —Jane Eyre, *Charlotte Brontë*

1.

Theocritus is more your bag than mine,
the classics a closed book. My darkest years
never as static as that — and who compares?
Who'd look to poetry to give the sign
or set the standard? Allusion, illusion:
even this 'Portuguese' is antique verse
too far removed in contours and figures
from what I want to write — as if a line
could draw a life! And yet the mystic Shape
hovers as always, palpable enough
to drag me in, and dare me to escape:
Guess now who holds you? I am no one's slave
nor mistress, I am style and turn and trope
that (w)ring the answer out: *Not Death, but Love.*

2.

But only three in all God's universe
hold us in place. Your word, my word, relied
upon, produce another, deified.
Too nebulous for darkness to disperse —

rather to deepen then, and burn. Who stirs
because we love — compelled — an ardent guide
we have brought forth like life from Adam's side.
Pantheists then, because our love confers
presence at every step, why fear an end?
Mountain and storm our warm familiars,
ocean in us, and death a vibrant friend —
Godhead is ours, and we're its avatars
reaching beyond ourselves, as suns transcend
their limit in an afterlife of stars.

3.
Unlike are we, unlike, O princely heart!
Those all alert to inequalities,
who wish to tear all bright things down to size,
look for a way to lever us apart —
one must oppress, the other pitch her art
by proxy, parasite. Our liberties
more than republican, don't recognise
regent or subject — only counterpart.
Playing at princes, we command our due,
no more, no less. In this variety
is strength, the same way metal formed of two
disparate parts gains durability.
If any crown, this alloy in which you
and I might overrule our destiny.

4.

You have your calling to some palace-floor
but choose to flout it for a cottage where
comforts are few, and company is rare.
When we have drawn the drapes and locked the door,
none of it matters. Those who fret and pore,
envious, at your record, who compare
their work to yours and count the world unfair —
what do they know of all that came before?
Valuing nothing, nothing can get in
but one another, habitation proof
against all weathers and what's worst within.
Love's most alive when seeming most aloof.
We build one flesh, and this our breathing skin
is all foundation, radiant walls and roof.

5.

What a great heap of grief lay hid in me
you were not first to feel, nor to discern
the scathing, helpless flares that still now burn
and drop to embers. Others slow to see
approached but soon drew back indignantly.
That these same flames which ravaged could in turn
fan into poem or passion, each would learn
no compensation, and take leave of me.
Only you stay, and love me. Not to tread
them out, but with your deepest breath to blow
my blind remaining light to life instead.
Nothing daunts you. The faithful man may go
into the furnace and be comforted;
you are annealed, and temper me also.

An Outing

It's the old argument of form and content,
whether our snowman has to look like that.
Medium none too amenable
so that we settle
for what it offers: rotund and slothful,
no family resemblance.

All we didn't mean to represent
bodied forth on a public path, no hat
or pipe to fix him in genre,
only the dubious honour
of a full belly, legs up as if in labour,
self-deliverance.

It looks like Mummy, the child cries, intent
on maintaining safe distance.

Keyhole

Point of entry matched
with point of loss,
your ghosted umbilicus,

discretion here poetic
in its aptness, tidily
hiding the new scar

inside the very first. You'd hardly
notice this one spot, deadlock
left upon exit

though sometimes it twinges
with sex, with stretching,
with lifting children,

where he nipped in
while you were out to it
and shut you off —

tubes as wayward
as thin blown glass
clamped and fashioned

to pure ornament,
minimalism
putting to shame

the baroque convolutions
of your reasoning,
your indecision.

Search

St Marylebone Cemetery was
a *suitable walk* for Edwardian children
even when Father and Boy lay restless
and so recently there —

some kind of sobering-up or
memento mori for
the daughter who'd nursed him through DTs,
the sister who'd seen him catch fire.

All through my childhood …
as a general exercise!

Now in turn I meander
        among the gone-before
    trying to catch a likeness
                or prove our distance.

                    *

Like any gathering this is addictive,
there might always be one more name or date
that would pin the thing, stop it bleeding,
real selvage.

                Instead,
this running mess, a mass of loose
threads, a text that can only unravel.

The public record
an illusion of points, of stitches,

but the stories   the contradictors
        the hearsay
letters transcribed and morphing,
the rumour-ridden heirlooms!

The constant correction
the play
the give
the tension.

The meaning of incompletion.

*

How in one house they could name
with such shades of variation:

Emma, Emily, Maria, Mary-Ann, Mary,
Emma-Ann

as if not discrete but
all on a spectrum —

what did a name mean
when you stayed all your life
in the place where your father's
father's father was born?

And each decade of census
I find one girl less
as she moves to the next house
taking her chances under new aegis
becoming *one flesh*

harder to track
so Protean!

Or Daphne-like,
lead-struck and wooden.

*

Yet I find my English
obscenely easily —
my Irish only from gravestones
and family hearsay

(which will have to do
in light of the waste laid
to census papers by government
by civil war
so many decades like chunks
dropping out of collective memory)

find them dispersed
how willingly?
if not as readily as dandelion
then pig melon kicked and split apart
scattered before the records
even start.

*

Henry Felix, it's dark
in the part of that century
where I fix you at last, clustered
with your wife and baby
named alike.
If we could speak I'd tell you
how many more to come
though perhaps not the one
who lives to fourteen only,
just long enough to show
on another census —
this hateful hindsight!
But my screen is a two-way mirror, I am
unthinkable. You're on your own here.
I like you this way: cellarman,
it says, new father, bare sketch
I can colour as you must have been
before you gave in,
or you couldn't have bred
your later boy
to be the high-spirited one
where the stories start,
raised him, as it happens,
only a few miles away
from my own grandmother,
on the north side of London
they will each one day leave
for a hard reason.

I see them passing
each other, unguessed, random,
though already they shoulder
the common future
of their children's children.
I would not intervene.

*

This facsimile located online
but ordered by phone
(wary of identity theft,
we don't shop on the net)

all the way from England, down
two centuries

interlaced with the next, tenuous
as daisy-chains, or slipping
wallpaper, when you try
to match a pattern —

foreshortens, distorts each life:
we witness birth and marriage
side by side, time collapsed; compare
the signatures, at once
insistently generic, of their age,
yet somehow enough *like Grandpa's,
like Nanna's,* to make us shiver —

beyond these
there is only the individual
parish register,
if you know the location,
the world before convergence,
the rush to centralise.

All except '**X**, Amelia, her mark'
reduced to an act of consent,
just as much in there but
uncoopted.

*

This link though live
leads nowhere, there are
too many of us and once you go
far enough, we are all connected
so the line means nothing

and this link, so tantalising —
now dead.

*

Grandma White née Toogood
who loved and fed and cared for
the Edwardian children —

left after Father
succumbed to his spirits

and Boy caught alight
at the nursery hearth
aged three

(the same details, in the same order
told in old age by each sister
in their respective countries
of emigration) —

Grandma White, we called her,
née Toogood, second wife
of Grandpa, and no relation,
does not show up on the record.

Neither of course does the maid
who was left to watch
in the nursery
that day

only fifteen

and who
anonymously
for more than a century
will wear the blame.

*

My fingers, these keys
grown tentacles,
grown tendrils, entangle
everywhere.

It's like pulling on gossamer
after the spider's
long gone,

or ectoplasm,

or gathering manna
so welcome when found but
gone the next morning.

I lock onto nothing substantial —

a little cold hand at the window
that turns to a tree
in a storm.

Legend

When my father expresses wonder at how
ultrasound let him watch
the clot in his leg, exactly
like the clot that killed his mother
decades ago — on his birthday, so he could never
mark age in quite the same way,

I tell him about Timmy at eight weeks,
a mouse-like huddle, and then
months later, a face in profile, and near the end
or beginning, a definite sex so the name
was settled on — I tell him because
there was no ultrasound
back in the days when his children —

me, I feel it now, among others —
were born, some in the same
hospital where he now lies sweating, his ankles
swollen but recognisably
the ones I also carry, varicose, *blue roses*
on hotter days,

he had to imagine us, from the outside,
like that, not known in his flesh
as a mother could, not pictured — he had to say us
to believe us, he could tell stories,
could ride to the birth-ward

on a scooter with the older kids
wedged behind him, but not be in on it,

could develop a belly
only from boozing till someone asked him,
Who's having the baby?
— could drink and drink as if something
needed flushing from his whole system,
some blockage needed thinning.

Now he is thin and puritan, the surface tension
of his skin uncertain,
like something disagreeing,
not settled. He has reached that age
when his peers are going,
one by one, like well-aimed blows,
the loss of a cylinder, an engine.

He is taking oxygen
for emphysema, and for blood, warfarin.
He is under instruction. He is at that stage
where you trade off risk of surgery
against time you have left anyway. He is amazed
by technologies, he forgets
his ills for a minute with each new surgical method
or gadget he tells me, child with a toy.

Ten years ago
when they put him on pethidine
during treatment for cancer, he slipped in and out
of cogency, reaching up to unlatch

a window that wasn't there, and weeping
when he knew it; or speaking whole chunks
of military history he'd once read
as we sat and chatted, then asking
Why am I saying that?

I have watched him
swerve and correct so many times
with machinic distance, thinking
he can survive anything, because he thought it, dogged,
and I always took my cues from him in thinking,
though I got chances
he never had, leaving school at fourteen.
I may not seem to have been much but I was a legend
he says, *a legend in the car business, and a legend*
in the insurance business too, and I remember
so many times that mantra
back in the days when he drank, as if he must say it
to clutch at something,

and whatever was at him then is at him
again now, but more totalitarian,
compelling,
like that time he made me stand at dawn
on the edge of the Bight, because he had seen it
so many times alone, that black water
where earth fell away.

Junction

Fox, you are overwritten.
Freeze-frame vision
too like a poem. I brake
and the children clamour,
noses to glass, chill mirror.

Languid, askance, at leisure —
slow motion that spells
disaster — so unlike
your usual flare and streak,
I have to check
for tail to reckon you.

Reckless, a matter of time.
Your beauty is none the less.
Your eyes fix mine as if
to guess at destination,
what brings us to this pass.

On our way to the nameless,
brazen as day, no truce,
no cover, marked man,
you appraise
and release us.

Intruder

Nagging away at rooftop like
something bothering the brain
I can't put my finger on.

Staking a hole with crowbar beak or
expanding what's already there.
I picture the rift, like a bite
from a cone upended, ooze
and stickiness. Icicles
weaken and drop. Whispers
like loose mice he lets in.

There's his precision,
tool or weapon, the fear of chinks:
wer knuspert an meinem Häuschen?
Der Wind ...
Shunts bed from bearings
glass from watercolour, outdoor
poltergeist. I'm on
borrowed time.

In here is no air.
In here is light, a tight
sort of inner radiance
I have given up for.
My parlour of authorless clatters.
This pallor.

Not flashy, no
ladderback, that
scarlet nape, the drape of
wide wings that flap as I
throw up the sash.
Five times to scare him off.
As if.

He merely grants respite,
retreating to distance,
indeterminate. He likes that.
His clack is a hacking laugh.
long jerky leash I'm on …
Nothing so certain
as he'll be back.

Identikit

Red bird who shadows me
from housetop to kitchen
I have you now

you match the field guide,
however static,
too exactly

to elude me for long —
hot flare in the bare
uppermost twigs or

blur in the snowy window,
fleeting as temper.
I didn't expect you here:

you are like anything
out of keeping.
I would fit in,

draw walls
around me like
the curtains missing

from every pane.
Instead, I should name you
loud and clear

twin to my own
red interior
be in here

as you are out there.

Raccoon

So you really do exist. Slowly cautious,
slumping by this window

wide as the screens where I've only
ever seen you till now

where I sit and sit and
cannot write —

you, foreign as inspiration
plodding as method.

Myopic, I take a moment to place you
plump as a homely cat and silent

thicker than fox and
masked in movement.

Now in focus, you evoke our numbat
and under threat — I hear

they call you *fur-bearer*
no wonder you go low-key

come without fuss
and leave no trace.

By the time I've fixed you
you're elsewhere, according

to your nature, hand-scratcher, trickster,
solitary visitor.

Redback

Whatever fails to stir
invites her —

sloth of a worn chair
rag mop left sunning
too long, Medusan,
basket of old washing
untouched paper

or even
those routes not taken
around the house.

Insidious with patience,
dumb immanence —
she tests my principle
so sure on the grand scale
weak on the small
— because I'm able? —

I say, *the children*,
that's fair enough
yet something else is
underneath,

each rock or chunk of wood
ready to turn weapon.

He says he doesn't know me
so hard, decided.

A decade, yet
unsounded.

I have my limits.

No unswept corner,
passive with silk and gossamer
of tripwire

no sitting still.

Dislocation

Wasp at the top of the house
spring's warmed, old oven —
we've both miscalculated.
O art of expectation!

Staggery, rag-imped thing.
All winter I came up
with nothing doing. Dead as a bone
and where were you then?

Always here, but hidden?
Little cancer in remission
buzz in the belfry;
the DDT, the mercury

blood won't be rid of,
this residue, like you
filming the walls till posters
peel down and the virgin desk

has a patina, a sleazy feel.
Even my tongue's dull,
festering. Get a glass
and catch you up

down all those flights because
the attic latch is stuck,
not flush,
no way out but descent.

Flung from the back door
you fail to take wing,
equivocal,
jewel in the wrong setting.

Curriculum Vitae

What are her weaknesses? Well, she's a writer, and writers will always
place their art above any other career, so don't expect her to put
the job first.
> — A referee (who needs enemies?)

Go back to school and get some nous.
> — Angry first boss, who was also a poet,
> and pronounced it to rhyme with 'louse'

Sessional, part-time, casual, fixed-term, adjunct, freelance, substitute,
Temping, cobbling, stretching, relieving, resting
Only ever euphemistically. In residence, meaning
Soon leaving. It never seemed real to me
But kept biting till I learned to stand back.
Narcissism, egotism, think the world owes you a living,
God's gift. Can't stick at anything. It rolled by
Like an in-flight movie, in snatches
Repeating and edited for a general audience,
With the sound dropped out, the invisible captain
Always interrupting: the *race*, the *course* of a life. Le train-train
Quotidien that made her stop eating. Métro boulot no go —
If she'd been a poet she could have justified it.
A series of workshops each winter, don't list the dates
It looks better when there are no gaps, though the one
Advantage of sexist assumptions
Is the woman can say, I was raising children.
Home duties. Self-employed. *I <u>was</u> working, I just didn't have a job.*

1.   *Rep*

Payoff was freebies: largesse
Of old-stock chocolate offloaded
On the children next door, who adored you for it, or stickers,
Display units, useless blow-up cushions
Blazoned with logos — but more, company car,
Clothing; training weekends
You stretched into holidays by coughing up the difference,
So your boys could run riot in a flash hotel.
Living for appearances. I met you
At this or that party-plan gathering, doing a favour
For a friend, because your time was *after all* your own.
You thought I needed brightening, some stuffing,
The gumption you'd had to drag up from somewhere
And must pass on, evangelist, everybody's angel,
The can-do lady. *I never worried*
About my size, it was only an obstacle
To others, and with the right colour consultant
And some clever tailoring, I scrub up pretty well.
I'll never be short of a dollar.

2.   *Courthouse*

Disbelief of the schoolyard mums
Who've taken you till now for altogether
Too louche and bohemian. You don't mention
You're only slicing envelopes, eternal junior
At thirty-five, filing
And photocopying in epic proportion:

Two hundred pages of someone proving
Why they must break up a young family
And *take into care* … Sick dummy
Of their compositing, you slap the pages down
Want to go home, but see it out. The bailiff
Rubs at his knuckles with relish
On collecting the daily file, and when all
Else dwindles, they get you writing
Infringements — handwriting —
On driver's licences whose names
You try not to register.
There's always a hand behind it,
And yours is neat if unskilled.
But you only come into your own
When an urgent court paper
Is found to be missing a final line,
Too late to reprint, and the boss
Says no one else is old enough
To remember the knack
Of the manual typewriter.

3.   Ride-on

After graduation with Honours
He went to Parks & Gardens:

It's great, I get to sit on the thing
And go round and round all day pretending
I haven't finished, and the dumb cunts
Pay me for it.

4. Begging the question

Poetry editor
On famous poet having personal problems
(A tautology):

I've always thought he'd be cured
If he only got himself a real job.

5. Housekeeper

Of diminishing economies:
Each week she returned
To the place, there was less
Of everything: the boys' clothes
Gone to that place only boys' clothes go
Like dogs' heaven, hopeful but never provable,
The iron burned out, the fridge
Reduced to one thawing lamb-corpse-lump
And she supposed to spin gold from straw.
Started bringing the veggies with her,
Spending her pay to earn her pay, feeling sorry
For the place she couldn't supply, the runaway
Mother who sent presents from exotic locations
But never a note. When the glass broke
On the panel by the front door, the dad said,
Just reach through the hole to let yourself in.

6. *Tour guide, colonial cottage*

Your pale face presenting like a cloudy mirror
And the ginger hair that clinched it under your bonnet
Unsettled us, would-be ancestress,
As much as the stream of words: each room
Pinned in historic context, verbatim.
No chance of looking around, ad lib.
We could hardly breathe.
It was past air coming up for another cycle
Moving through us, disposable:
All the same to you.
Every day a dress rehearsal, repetition
Compulsion: poetaster,
Misfit. Inside,
We were anachronism, and you ruled,
Patient with failure to assimilate,
Correcting assumptions like the swerve
Of a child's hoop,
Pushing us on till at last we came out
Where we had entered, and the bright light
Brought back to us another life we hadn't been to yet.

7. Bookseller

A bookseller has become the first blogger in Britain to be sacked
from his job because he kept an online diary in which he
occasionally mentioned bad days at work and satirised his
'sandal-wearing' boss. —The Guardian, *Jan 12, 2005*

Can you be sacked for a poem too?
It was a genre he drew on, and only the real thing
If he let himself feel it on their time, caricature
The last refuge of the bled. I felt I knew him,
Any of them, interchangeable
Though not in the way the bosses think
But in their responses: you grow into what you do.
Some with degrees that turned out useless
Or even PhDs, settling for meagre pay
Outside their field
And some for thirty years
Who'd brewed such bile they took it out
On hapless customers:
Do you have this book?
No. And turned away. Smugly redeemed,
Some power, somewhere. Refuge of intellect
Without resources, without room to move.
But huge compensations: books, and books,
And books, and special discounts, and first look-in
When stock's discarded. Teabreaks
Where no one minds you reading. It's the perks
They get you with, and once they do, you're got.

We never saw the bosses, except
The day they came to tell us the firm was sold
And only some of us would keep our jobs
In the new dispensation.
Each one in solidarity
Rolling eyes but inwardly calculating
Whether or not we were crucial. A joke,
No. But lots of laughter. *You gotta laugh or you'd cry.*
A loose, informal bond.
Back when I'd started, I was warned
By the daughter of the daughter of a Communist
If you ask about unions, they shift you to the warehouse
And you're never seen again.
So many of us dispersed across the chain, this could be true —
But that day, when the bosses came,
The whole crowd pulled together,
Branch upon branch shrunk into the main store
To hear the pronouncement
Like the meek who inherit the earth in some other life.

Greensleeves

        And who but my lady
ever affable
        in laying down the law
handing out typing
        with immaculate tact
so neat it scarcely needed
        the transmuting

polite in her blonde-topped cool-suit
        and young-professional distance
plucking the occasional
                        office-girl to attend
some conference
                — *improving our assets*
as she told the Big Boss, to excuse the day off.

Once it was me and another.
                        She was very Proper,
setting us to the right and left of her,
                        commanding notes.
Lunch together
                like a teacher's favour, telling us
about her husband,
                life back in England.

The only moment:
                and then it was all routine again

except for a novel
                she dropped in with the next day's copy

I thought you might enjoy this

a lesbian sci-fi comical romp
which I duly read
                on my own time, of course

and returned to her

        like a fixed glitch
        a tipp-exed question
        I could not decipher —

with the typing
                which she never complained of.

Infusion

Unreadable, these cups
she'd fill each night and steep
to prolong the last moment
before you'd part.

Nothing to ruffle sleep,
trouble the airy step
that took two stairs

at a leap, no looking back,
you in the dark well.
She'd choose the type,

wipe each bowl
till it shone up
moonwhite to her own
superior light,

before pouring
just so much
pure heat, all promise

but evanescent —
then chide at the way you held it
not quite *comme il faut*

scalding the hand, the palate
yet you followed, you followed
all the way up, and did not sip
but drank deep.

Passionfruit

The faintest trace on fingers
and we know you
instantly, by scent

and that's just the outside,
belle-laide,

elaborate
as a Fabergé egg

useless really to feed us —

pure aesthetics
tangled there
on the bare fence,

basking in the same sun
as concrete, asbestos

where it glances off
but you are absorption

light transmuted
to elusive dulcet
concentration,

time biding,
we watch you drop
unapprehended,

purple patches
in the baldest story.

Inside your chamber
a viscous lining —
it feels like thieving —
resistant sac,

the truth of the matter,
thing-in-itself

without purpose
save to draw out
the essence of other things

grace note and garnish,
pitted mnemonic,
philosopher's stone,

bittersweet
encapsulation.

Vigil

Rowethorpe Nursing Home

Your eyes still light upon the world below,
being now all that moves. Each breath hard won,
none of us knows how long there is to go.

Now even meals are highlights in the slow
dull leached-out days, until you see someone.
Your eyes still light upon the world below

new to you now as twenty years ago
when all was at beck and call, that's now undone.
None of us knows how long there is to go

before we hit the impasse. Your hello
shrugs off the decades: *I knew you would come.*
Your eyes still light upon the world below,

insisting it's no surprise, these words so low
I strain to catch them, nursing every one.
None of us knows how long there is to go.

A snatch of static on the radio,
a dazzled squint into imagined sun.
Your eyes still light upon the world below;
none of us knows how long there is to go.

A Deposition

... the conviction that Fate was of stone,
and Hope a false idol — blind, bloodless,
and of granite core
        — Villette, Charlotte Brontë

Twenty years since I crashed into you
or was driven. Directionless.
Monument, you commanded the view.
Tree and sky fell into place

for you, driven; directionless,
I made a fear to meet my fate.
Tree and sky fell into place,
like stone no gloss could palliate

I made a fear to meet my fate:
Landlocked Colossus
no Christian gloss could palliate,
cold Ozymandias.

Landlocked Colossus
weak at the knee you bent to pray,
cold Ozymandias
where all that remain are feet of clay.

Weak at the knee you bent to pray:
inconceivable you should fall
where all that remain are feet of clay
out of the wreckage at last to crawl.

Inconceivable you should fall,
monument — you commanded the view.
Out of the wreckage at last I crawl
Twenty years since I crashed into you.

Mnemonic

As if for the last time

looking, as if sight were fixative
but to what end, having moved on
so often now I have forgotten

to feel selfsame, the last time frost
on broken cornfields, light of spring
subsequent but without sense

for the nowhere-belonging.
Just when you meant
to become someone you melt

like that teetering bank and only the melt
will register, not the particular:
a poem half-got

fingers misleading the keyboard I quit
in childhood but believing
they have it

lost and retained as a mother-tongue
in which the word *your*
might have one syllable, or more,

can you hear me? Here, by the mismatched
vinyl and odd boxes, detritus
of the part-timer's office,

whose details
will lose me
in a month, six months,

slippery as syntax —
you-all will be there but meaningless
as an empty rhyme scheme.

You shall have no other fabric before me

Slippery as mercury

Just as untouchable

I split and multiply

Give back your likenesses

Which are legion

How you rule and specify

To placate me, distant

As the skirt of a Lady

You may never accost

Hoist and fly

Down to my last inch

That must never approach

The ground, until the day

Of dignity

When I lie down with you

Should you win favour

Union at head

And left shoulder

And grace the whole length of you

Elegy

Reel

Two nights after you died I dreamt of newsreels
playing as if now — the Germans
were banning all strangers
from taking trains, and language
was the test. We were running
from the trains, but they made us sit
once again through the newsreel, this time
Italian fascists, and my newfound dream-friend,
twin-friend,
the only one I'd ever had
failed to take up her seat
in the musty cinema. They told me
she'd been crushed by vegetation, by matter
encroaching and abundant, like some fifties
disaster movie where you fight off
giant Nature. Lost
as soon as found.
      I dream around you,
not of you, I never did —
always allusion, ellipsis. Little histories
collapsing, a confusion of heydays,
roman à clef.

This is persistence of vision, this stubborn
use of second person
with content lost, perverse attachment
of a verb like the one Stendhal muses
has such limited conjugation.
And yet I died too.
Noli me tangere
still in a state of transition,
not knowing who I'll be.

Total immersion

You lowered me
backwards and I gave way.
If I'd lifted my eyes the sky
was glassy and open
to interpretation, but I chose to
look inward.

You stood
assassin of old man, midwife
to new

forced me under
like those blind puppies

but I came back
for more

till that my *garments, heavy with their drink*
had to be cast aside

Raised me, one-handed,
an image.

Coldest shoulder

Again you turn your back on me
but this time it's final,

and the same old impotence
has me rocking, wordless

digging for nerve-ends.
You must be in there,

in me somewhere —
but they have removed you,

tumour, anomaly,
you multiply —
give me catatonic
any day;

the stillness of madness
but not absence.

Kept back

The lines are running away
like self unravelling

I thought intact
all these years

could not staunch them

I shirk, screen-shy, would revert
to pen and paper

relief of friction
'*delicate self-cutting*'

anything
anything

The sourness knowing
the worst will be over
a matter of days

the merciless privacy
of grief that won't let anyone out
till someone owns up.

Exegetical

Now I have given up on poetry
no longer confident
it can purge me
or provide.

These are its annotations:
the text itself has disappeared
internal logic
can reconstruct

only minimally —
there was never a source,
there is no one to gloss,

no audience.

Inscription

Lavish and jagged as lightning, a hand
too clean for a man's, deadly accurate.
I had now and then
one line of it, under a ream
of cold typescript, of circular — you knew
it would give too much of you,
striking the same place twice — you stinted,
you measured it out, hot linctus,
hard liquor. King of the underscore,

between the lines, the lacuna.
I would devour it now like the scroll
of Revelation, sweet to the mouth
but turning the stomach sour
if I could find one letter
in all this upheaval:
snowdrifts of paper settle, a mass
of old skin cells, of scattered ash.

Heretical

I lay in hospital
and waited

upheld by drips and straps, my head
surveying the post-lapsarian world
of my body

finding it not so good

still functioning as if
it would never miss me,

saying at heart *there is no god*
there is no god —

waited
for one who didn't come
on principle.

Tomb objects

Each little gift you took and never
remarked on, a piece
in this sick mosaic,
now crumbling:

I want them back now,
like letters but cryptic,
no currency.

I fear their circulation, headless,
footless, tossed

like a ball intercepted
by the careless,
or curious,
but you have doubtless dropped them
along the wayside

Hansel's crumbs
for birds to glut on

removing all traces.

Interview

Coldly polite
when I married him
as if I had the right

you on edge
of sofa, proffering tea
that wasn't had,
wife by side

and us facing:
clockwork figures
telling the weather
against each other.

Why bring him there?
Wet, bedraggled, a cat
limping in with its victim,

small corpse of cathexis
messing the carpet

where once I sat
at your feet, and you
accepted that.

You cut to the chase:
'If you died
tonight and God asked

Why should I let you in
to heaven ...?'

— infallible question meant
to sort out the unregenerate —

his answer didn't fit: 'here
I am the way you made me;
do what you want.'

Any man's death

Landslide I felt
every bit as much
as if it were never predicted

(felt like Christ
when the woman touched
and drained him

as if his nerves extended
to the very hem of his garment)

we, continent
subject to ebb and flow
sense the minutest loss,

were never divided
but by this shouldering mass
that insists and insists

on claiming us, matrix
of bitterness,
salt-cold mouth

devouring Norfolks, house
by house by coastal road,
a whole yard

downed overnight,
towering chimney
that was once an inland well,

fight or
flight to interior,
'managed retreat'.

Recovery

You have been cut away
like wreckage from which I am
extracted, metal that echoes
pins and stitching, my reconstruction.
An ache, a splinter, a vanished hand,
a ringing no one else can hear,
a tinnitus, a voice
that is still.

After

I remember you, Shapeshifter, you did this
after my brother and from then on
after anyone who went, you strutted about
making your mockeries, tilt of a cheek,
a gait, hunch, waistline, back of a neck,
a gesture, making us think, for a minute,
they were still out there — impersonator, headfucker,
is that all you can come up with?
Hanging around to rub it in?
Your taunts liltless as bad Latin,
you ancient, you po-mo performative, nothing
but lip-synch no public would fall for. I can
assure you, you don't even
come close.

First published 2008 by
FREMANTLE PRESS
25 Quarry Street, Fremantle
(PO Box 158, North Fremantle 6159)
Western Australia.
www.fremantlepress.com.au

Copyright © Tracy Ryan, 2008.

This book is copyright. Apart from any fair dealing for the purpose
of private study, research, criticism or review, as permitted under the
Copyright Act, no part may be reproduced by any process without
written permission. Enquiries should be made to the publisher.

Consultant Editor Wendy Jenkins.
Cover Designer Tracey Gibbs.
Cover photograph by Nemanja Glumac.
Printed by Everbest Printing Company, China.

National Library of Australia
Cataloguing-in-publication data

Ryan, Tracy, 1964– .
Scar revision.

ISBN 9789213610671 (pbk.).

I. Title.

A821.3